AVAILABLE NOW
from Lerner Publishing Services!

The *On the Hardwood* series:

Boston Celtics
Brooklyn Nets
Chicago Bulls
Dallas Mavericks
Houston Rockets
Indiana Pacers
Los Angeles Clippers
Los Angeles Lakers

Miami Heat
Minnesota Timberwolves
New York Knicks
Oklahoma City Thunder
Philadelphia 76ers
Portland Trail Blazers
San Antonio Spurs
Utah Jazz

COMING SOON!

Additional titles in
the *On the Hardwood* series:

Atlanta Hawks
Cleveland Cavaliers
Denver Nuggets
Detroit Pistons
Golden State Warriors
Memphis Grizzlies
Phoenix Suns
Washington Wizards

To Order • www.lernerbooks.com • 800-328-4929 • fax 800-332-1132

ON THE HARDWOOD

PETE BIRLE

On the Hardwood: Boston Celtics

Copyright © 2014
by Pete Birle

Printed in the United States of America.

MVP Books
2255 Calle Clara
La Jolla, CA 92037

MVP Books is an imprint of Book Buddy Digital Media, Inc., 42982 Osgood Road, Fremont, CA 94539

MVP Books publications may be purchased for educational, business, or sales promotional use.

Cover and layout design by Jana Ramsay
Copyedited by Susan Sylvia
Photos by Getty Images

ISBN: 978-1-61570-848-2 (Library Binding)
ISBN: 978-1-61570-832-1 (Soft Cover)

TABLE OF CONTENTS

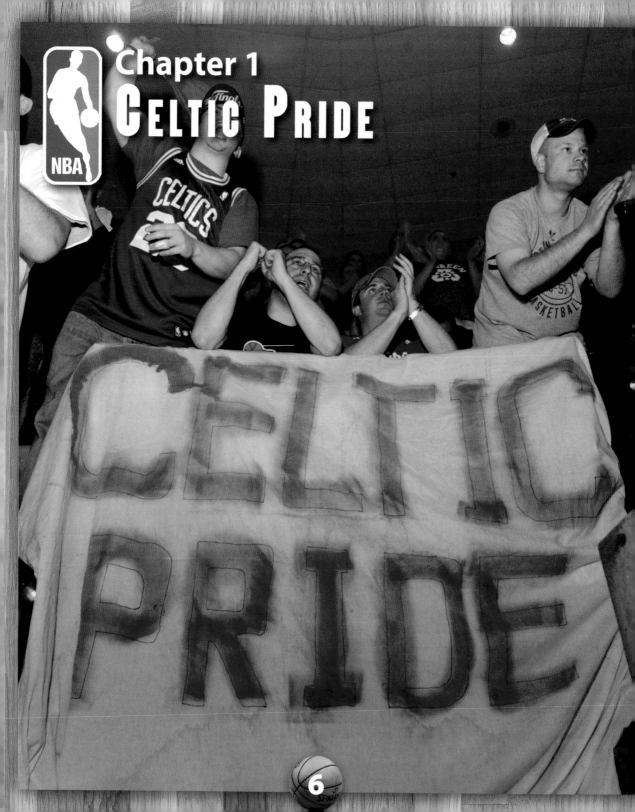

Chapter 1

CELTIC PRIDE

The city of Boston, Massachusetts, holds a unique position in America as the cradle of liberty and the birthplace of freedom. It was the citizens of Boston who protested against Britain and started the chain of events that led to the American Revolution.

Boston also lays claim to another unique position. It is the cradle of championships and the birthplace of professional basketball.

Glance up at the ceiling of the TD Garden in Boston someday, and you'll see why. Once inside the home of the Boston Celtics, you'll appreciate a view like none other in the National Basketball Association.

Hanging from the rafters are the Celtics' many banners honoring their NBA-record 17 championships. Alongside is a banner identifying the Celtics' retired jerseys, worn by some of the greatest players in the history of the game. In fact, the Celtics have retired 21 numbers, the most of

The original State House in Boston, site of the Boston Massacre, is one reason why Boston is known as the cradle of liberty. The city is also the birthplace of professional basketball.

The Celtics acknowledge their ties to the large Irish-American population in Boston by having a shamrock as its symbol.

any professional sports franchise in North America.

When you play for the Celtics (or coach them), you become part of the league's—and the sport's—history. The Celtics have a record of success that spans nearly 70 years. They have won titles in five different decades. It is more fact than opinion: Basketball and Boston are one and the same.

In their green and white uniforms, the team—and its name, Celtics—honor the large number of Irish immigrants who settled in "Beantown." The team also has a shamrock as its symbol and a

The Best of the Best
The Boston Celtics have retired more numbers (21) than any other professional sports franchise in North America.

leprechaun as its mascot. Lucky the Leprechaun is leaning on his Irish cane, or "shillelagh," (pronounced shih-lay-lee), spinning a basketball on his index finger and winking. It's like he knows something we don't. One of the most recognizable mascots in all of sports, Lucky shows confidence, arrogance, and a little bit of mischief. Just like the Celtics and the city they call home.

The Celtics have done much more than just win championships, though. They have developed what fans in Boston call "Celtic Pride," a style and approach that has defined the franchise since its beginning.

For one, Boston has always stressed playing team basketball. In fact, no Celtic has ever won an NBA scoring title. They have been successful blending different players, from different backgrounds, with different roles, into a solid unit,

Lucky the Leprechaun—confident, arrogant, and mischievous—is the Boston Celtics' mascot.

9

No "I" in Team

The Celtics have always stressed team basketball with an approach that has come to be known as "Celtic Pride."

no matter who is coaching them.

As a result, the Celtics are known for having lovable role players step up with the game on the line. Usually, it would happen in the old Boston Garden, perhaps the most famous NBA arena in history. The Garden had no air conditioning; but it did have a unique parquet (par-kay), or square-patterned, floor. Over the years, the court developed numerous "dead spots," where a ball just might not bounce; every Celtic knew their location by heart. Of course, their opponents didn't. When the Celtics moved to the Fleet Center in 1995, they took the floor with them.

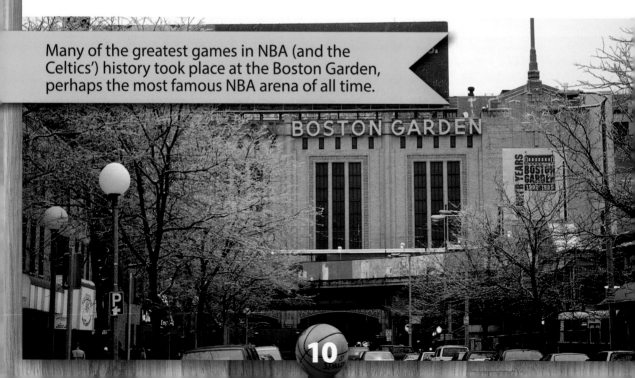

Many of the greatest games in NBA (and the Celtics') history took place at the Boston Garden, perhaps the most famous NBA arena of all time.

BOSTON GARDEN

Whether it was the system, the players, the floor, or Lucky the Leprechaun, it all came together once again in 2008. The Celtics went 66-16 in the regular season and won their 17th championship—and first in 22 years.

The matchup was between Boston and their long-standing rivals, the Los Angeles Lakers, who have just one fewer NBA title (16) than Boston. The two clubs, the most successful teams in NBA history, last met in the Finals in 1987. The 2008 NBA finals marked the 11th time the teams had faced off for the championship, with the Celtics winning eight of the previous 10 series.

The Celtics' "Big Three" of Paul Pierce, Kevin Garnett, and Ray Allen had been formed the previous summer to bring the title back to Boston. They had already helped accomplish the largest single-season turnaround in NBA history. By going 66-16 in the regular season, the Celtics registered a 42-game improvement from 2006 to 2007.

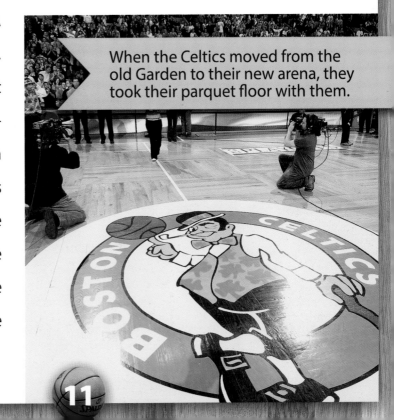

When the Celtics moved from the old Garden to their new arena, they took their parquet floor with them.

Hard Road to the Top

By the time Game 6 of the 2008 Finals had arrived, the Celtics were playing in their 26th game that postseason, an NBA record.

No team had to work harder for a championship than the Celtics in 2008. When Game 6 of the Finals arrived, they were playing in their record 26th postseason game. But up three games to two, they closed things out against Kobe Bryant and the Lakers in style. With the Garden faithful shouting "Beat L.A." and "Seven-teen," the Celtics blew out L.A., 131-92. The 39-point victory was the largest margin of victory ever in a championship-clinching game.

Garnett dominated with 26 points and 14 rebounds. Allen tied the single-game Finals record by nailing seven three-pointers. Rajon

The Celtics trio of Paul Pierce, Kevin Garnett, and Ray Allen had been formed to bring the title back to Boston.

Rondo put up 21 points, dished out eight assists, snagged seven rebounds and recorded six steals. And Pierce, who suffered a sprained knee in Game 1, captured Finals MVP honors by averaging 19.7 points, 5.0 rebounds and 4.6 assists.

Rajon Rondo showed why he is one of the best guards in the league with his performance over the Lakers in Game 6 of the 2008 Finals.

"It feels so great," said Pierce. "I'm not living under the shadows of the other [Celtic] greats now. I'm able to make my own history with my time here. If I was going to be one of the best Celtics ever to play, I had to put up a banner. And we did that.

"Who cares who gets the last shot or scores the most points? Who cares who gets the credit?" he added, speaking like a true Celtic. "If we win, we're all winners."

And that goes for everyone— from the front office, to the coach, to the players… and to the city of Boston.

Earning His Place

In helping Boston return to glory in 2008, Paul Pierce earned a spot among the Celtic greats. "To climb all the way to the top, this is a dream come true."

Chapter 2

Red, Russell, and Rings

Back in 1946, America's men in uniform had just returned home from fighting—and achieving victory—in World War II. The country was looking for some activities to enjoy in their post-war leisure. Walter Brown, president of the original Boston Garden, led a group of owners to start a professional basketball league.

Brown formed the Celtics to represent the city of Boston in the new Basketball Association of America. The BAA evolved into the NBA in the fall of 1949, with the Celtics as a charter member.

The Celtics were coming off four

Red Auerbach, who would often light his cigar on the bench, built the greatest dynasty in NBA history.

losing seasons, when Brown hired 32-year-old New Yorker, Arnold "Red" Auerbach, in 1950. A coach in the military during the war, Auerbach was an outspoken task master, who demanded excellence from his players by stressing team basketball. He ran all the practices, did all the scouting and scheduled all the team's road trips. With his trademark cigar clamped between his teeth, Auerbach did things his way. He would even light his cigar on the bench during games, once he thought the Celtics had things well in hand—which was often long before the game was over.

Auerbach was the architect of pro basketball's ultimate winning machine, orchestrating the greatest dynasty in sports history. It started with his acquisition of Bob Cousy, a flashy guard from Holy Cross in Worcester, Mass. Auerbach initially refused to draft Cousy, considering him not ready for big-time basketball. After the Chicago Stags folded,

The wins started to pile up once Bob Cousy, the best dribbler and passer in the league, joined the Celtics.

Boston won the rights to sign Cousy by pulling his name out of a hat.

Auerbach quickly learned that Cousy was the best dribbler and passer in the league. So he built a fast-break offense around the Hall of Famer, who led the NBA in assists eight times. For the next 16 years, the Celtics never had a losing record. But Boston failed to make the NBA Finals in their first 10 years of existence. That all changed in 1956 with Auerbach's brilliant trade and acquisition of 6'9" center Bill Russell.

Russell had just finished playing in the 1956 Olympics in Australia.

It was Bill Russell, the NCAA champion from the University of San Francisco, who turned the Celtics into champions.

Although the Harlem Globetrotters wanted Russell to become the next "Clown Prince of Basketball," Auerbach convinced him to play for the Celtics.

Previously, he led the University of San Francisco to 26 straight wins and the 1955 and 1956 NCAA titles. The Celtics weren't the only team interested in Russell. The Harlem Globetrotters, the exhibition basketball team that featured great hoop skills and comic routines, also wanted him. However, Auerbach convinced Russell to join him in Boston.

A top-notch defender and shot-blocker, Russell was perfect for the fast break. The recipe for Boston's success usually began with Russell clearing the boards and firing an outlet pass to Cousy. It usually finished with a layup by Bill Sharman, Sam Jones, or Tommy Heinsohn.

The Celtics won their first NBA championship in Russell's rookie year. Over the next 12 seasons, the Celtics captured an additional 10 rings—eight of which were in a row, the longest streak of consecutive championships in U.S. professional sports history. Five of those championships came against the Lakers. And Boston usually got the best of the Philadelphia 76ers, too, as Russell often outplayed his archrival, 7'2"

Tommy Heinsohn, who later coached the Celtics to a pair of NBA titles, was a hard-nosed player with a soft shooting touch.

Wilt "the Stilt" Chamberlain. (To show clearly whom he thought was the better player, Auerbach paid

Russell a salary of $100,001—one dollar more than what Chamberlain was earning in Philadelphia.)

Russell proved to be the most dominant defensive presence the league has ever seen. By the time he retired, he had hauled down a total of 21,620 rebounds, an average of 22.5 per game. He once pulled down 51 boards in a game and had 12 straight years with over 1,000 rebounds.

But he wasn't always the most popular player with fans around the league. Russell had a reputation for being focused solely on doing his job: playing basketball.

"I can honestly say that I have never worked to be liked," Russell said. "I have worked only to be respected."

In 1980, Russell was awarded the respect he sought. The Professional Basketball Writers Association of America voted Russell the Greatest Player in the History of the NBA—and Auerbach the greatest coach.

"The Celtic dynasty provided an anchor for the league," said Cousy. "I

Russell and the Celtics usually came out ahead in their match-ups with the Philadelphia 76ers.

don't think you'll ever see a run like that again."

Added Auerbach: "We liked to play, we liked to win, and we liked to have fun. That's what made it work for so long… It was really a family."

That's the way it was in the 1950s and 1960s, and even after Auerbach had turned the reins of the team over to player-coach Russell. It was the same in the 1970s, when Hall of Famer and all-time Celtics' scoring leader John Havlicek led the team to a pair of additional titles.

"The Celtics aren't a team," Auerbach once said. "They're a way of life."

And life was about to get even better.

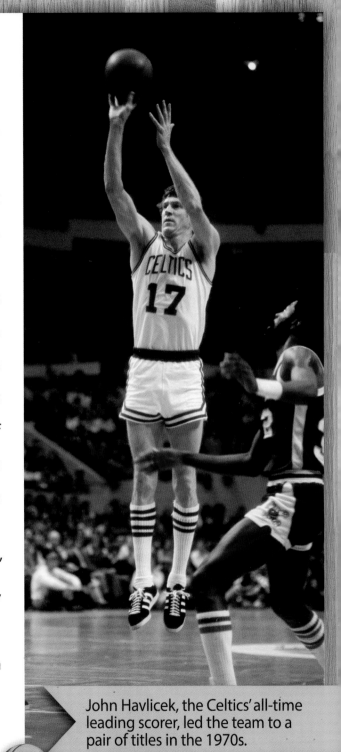

John Havlicek, the Celtics' all-time leading scorer, led the team to a pair of titles in the 1970s.

The Celtics owned two of the top eight picks in the 1978 NBA Draft. Auerbach took a risk and selected junior 6'9" Larry Bird of Indiana State with the sixth pick. He knew Bird would remain in college for his senior year, but the Celtics retained his rights for one year (a rule that has since changed). Bird signed with Boston soon after leading the Sycamores to the NCAA championship game, where they fell to Earvin "Magic" Johnson and the Michigan State Spartans.

Bird and his rivalry with Magic—not to mention the Celtics' rivalry with the Lakers—literally saved the NBA. (The two of them arguably attracted millions of fans.) Bird meant even more to the Celtics. The 1979-80 Rookie of the Year and three-time

NBA MVP also helped Boston reach the Finals five times and capture three more championships.

Amazingly, Bird did not attract any recruiters until his senior year of high school. He grew up in rural French Lick, Indiana, a town with less than 2,000 residents that had

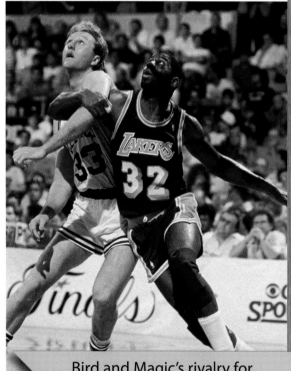

Bird and Magic's rivalry for the ages saved an NBA that needed a boost.

Bird grew up in French Lick, Indiana, a country town that loved the city game.

fallen on hard times. Not wanting to leave his home state, Bird made a deal with Louisville coach Denny Crum that if he beat the coach in a game of "Horse," he would not have to visit the school in Kentucky. The sharp-shooting Bird won easily and crossed Louisville off his list.

Bird did sign with Indiana University, having been courted by legendary coach Bobby Knight. When he got to Bloomington, he was on his own for the first time, too poor to go out on the town with his teammates. He lasted all of 24 days on campus. Without saying a word to anyone, including his coach, Bird hitchhiked back to French Lick.

He took a job for the town— cutting trees, painting street signs, sweeping roads, collecting garbage and unplugging sewers. While everyone else figured he was a lost cause, Indiana State kept after him. Not long after, he was battling Magic Johnson for the NCAA crown on a national stage.

What If...?

After leaving Indiana University, Larry Bird went back home to work. Had he not been pursued by Indiana State, he may have ended up working in his hometown for the rest of his life.

Nicknamed "The Hick from French Lick," Bird was everything Magic wasn't. ("Hick" is urban slang for someone from the country.) When he arrived in Boston, the quiet and reserved Bird had trouble adjusting to life in the big city—and being in a spotlight bigger and brighter than any he had experienced before.

When the rest of the team went out for a steak dinner, Bird stayed home, content to cut his grass. After a while, he drew quite a crowd mowing his lawn, as everyone wanted to get close to him.

Few played the small forward position like he did, with his shooting, ball-handling, and passing ability. Bird was at his best drawing the defense out, making it look as though he would shoot, before finally delivering a pinpoint pass to a teammate. Auerbach considered him the greatest basketball player of all time.

"Watching Larry Bird play became a privilege. Dazed basketball fans wandered around asking themselves, 'What wonderful thing did I ever do to deserve this?'" wrote

While a phenomenal shooter, Bird was at his best dishing out amazing assists.

Bird, Parish and McHale were known as the "Big Three," called the greatest frontcourt in the history of the game.

Boston sportswriters Bob Ryan and Terry Pluto.

Determined to craft a championship team around Bird, Auerbach orchestrated a pre-draft trade in 1980 that some consider the most lopsided in NBA history. He dealt the top pick (and one other first-round pick) to Golden State for 7'1" center Robert Parish, and the Warriors' top pick. Auerbach used that pick to draft 6'11" power forward Kevin McHale from the University of Minnesota.

"The Big Three" went on to play 12 seasons together. They won three championships, and were considered one of the greatest frontcourts in the history of the game. In 1996, a panel of media members, former players and coaches, and current and former team executives selected the NBA's Top 50 Players in History. Bird, McHale, and Parish all made the list.

Parish was a country boy, like Bird, only he was from Shreveport, Louisiana. He played in relative obscurity in his hometown at Centenary College, which had been sanctioned by the NCAA for violations. As a result, not only were the Gents banned from post-season play, but Parish's statistics were excluded from the NCAA's press guides. Although the school recognizes his feats on the court, the NCAA doesn't. His name is not in the record books. But it didn't matter. NBA scouts knew about him and what he could do.

By the time he got to Boston, he was known for his defense and

Robert Parish, at 7'1", ruled the paint for the Celtics for 14 years.

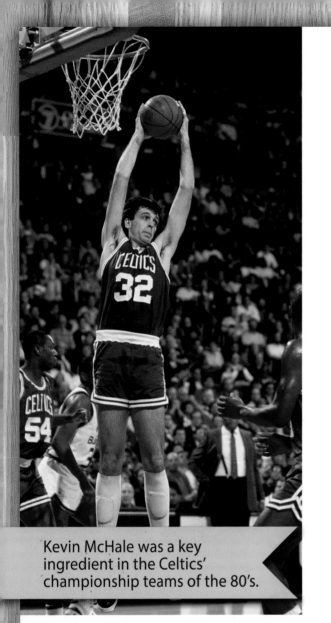

Kevin McHale was a key ingredient in the Celtics' championship teams of the 80's.

dropping through the hoop. In the end, Parish ruled the paint for the Celtics for 14 years. He retired having played more seasons (21) than anyone in NBA history.

"He's probably the best medium-range shooting big man in the history of the game," said Hall of Famer Bill Walton, Parish's backup during the Celtics' 1986 championship season.

In McHale, the Celtics found a player with a body made for basketball. With incredibly long arms and legs, McHale became one of the best inside players the game has ever seen. He used drop steps, head fakes, pump fakes, baby jump hooks, shovel shots and fadeaway J's to frustrate the league's best defenders.

ability to finish the fast break. But he was worshipped by the fans for a jump shot that seemed to skim the banners atop the Garden before

"He became the most difficult low-post player to defend—once he made the catch—in the history of the league," said former NBA coach Hubie Brown. "He was totally unstoppable because of his quickness ... and the long arms that gave him an angle to release the ball over a taller man or more explosive jumper."

McHale came from a small town in the remote Iron Range of northeastern Minnesota. A hockey player when he arrived at high school, he soon experienced a growth spurt that surprised his 5'10" father and 5'6" mother. It wasn't long before he hung up his skates for a pair of high-tops.

The 1980s Celtics' rosters were loaded with talent. There

were Hall of Famers Nate "Tiny" Archibald and Dennis Johnson, as well as Cedric Maxwell, M.L. Carr, Bill Walton and Danny Ainge. They won it all in 1981 vs. the Houston

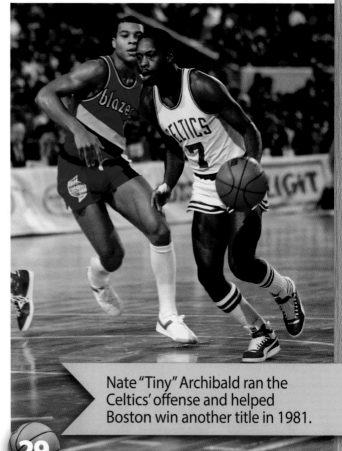

Nate "Tiny" Archibald ran the Celtics' offense and helped Boston win another title in 1981.

29

Rockets. They did it again three years later, in a matchup for the ages. It was Boston vs. Los Angeles, Bird vs. Magic, blue-collar Boston basketball vs. Hollywood's "Showtime." New coach K.C. Jones rallied the Celtics from a 2-1 deficit. Boston forced the Lakers to commit 31 turnovers in Game 4, and the Celtics earned an overtime victory.

Game 5 belonged to Boston—in 97-degree heat in the Garden. Players on both teams needed oxygen. Even one of the refs fainted from dehydration.

"Everybody talks about Boston having a leprechaun, but I always thought that leprechaun's name was Red," said Magic. He was referring to the notion that Auerbach may have been responsible for the Garden's air conditioning not working.

Larry Bird, who did not give out many compliments, said Dennis Johnson was "the best" he'd played with.

The Lakers got the best of the Celtics two other times in the NBA Finals during the 1980s. But in beating LA in seven games in 1984, Bird—who added Finals MVP to his regular-season MVP award—got revenge on Magic for his loss in college.

"I finally got him," Bird said of the player who challenged him the most. "I finally got Magic."

There were other "magic" moments for Boston during the Bird era, like the 1985-86 championship Celtics. They went 40-1 at home and are considered one of the best teams in NBA history. And there was

When Bird's Celtics beat Johnson's Lakers in 1984, Bird finally got revenge for his loss to Magic in the 1979 NCAA championship.

A Sixth Sense
One of Bird's greatest talents was his ability to anticipate his opponents' moves. His steal in the 1987 Eastern Conference Finals displayed his incredible instincts.

also Game 5 of the 1987 Eastern Conference Finals.

Defending champion Boston looked defeated. The young, tough Detroit Pistons had them tied 2-2 and were about to win to send the series back to Detroit. Up by one with just seconds to go, the Pistons fell victim to Lucky the Leprechaun. As Detroit's Isiah Thomas looked to pass the ball in from the sideline, Bird noticed that the Pistons' captain made eye contact with center Bill Laimbeer in the low post. So Bird cut into the passing lane and stole the ball before it could get to Laimbeer.

While he appeared to be headed out of bounds, Bird somehow managed to gather his balance at the baseline and turn toward the court. He spotted teammate Dennis Johnson heading down the lane.

One of the Celtics' greatest plays was in Game 5 of the 1987 Eastern Conference Finals. Bird saved a ball from going out of bounds and hit Johnson with a pass that DJ laid in for the last-second win.

Bird fired a pass to DJ, who promptly laid it in with one second remaining for a 108-107 victory.

In making the steal, Bird's instincts were phenomenal. But his ability to turn it into the winning basket made the play one of the greatest in playoff history. The Celtics went on to win the series in seven games and advance to the NBA Finals for the fourth year in a row (only to lose to the Lakers).

"I've always considered myself a pretty confident person, but I've never seen anyone who believed in himself like Larry did," said Ainge, the current Celtics' GM.

"There are times when you get it going and you are in this incredible place, this zone, where you are controlling the game," said Bird. "You feel no matter what you try, it's going to work. It's the greatest feeling in the world, because no one can stop you."

Bird once grabbed the rebound on his own missed shot, switched the ball from his right to his left in midair, and hit nothing but net.

Chapter 4
THE "BOSTON THREE PARTY"

ird was ultimately stopped, by a bad back. He retired in 1992. McHale retired in 1993. And Parish finally called it quits in 1994, at the age of 43. But even before that, it seemed as though Lucky the Leprechaun had gone on vacation.

Owners of the second overall pick in 1986, the Celtics drafted first-team All-American Len Bias of the University of Maryland. But the 6'8" Bias, whom Reebok signed immediately to a $3 million-dollar sneaker deal, died 48 hours after the draft from a drug overdose.

Then, 6'7" Reggie Lewis, who was seen as Bird's successor as the team's franchise player, died at the age of 27 from a heart attack in an off-season workout in 1993. Lewis was an enormously popular Celtic, due to the fact he played his college ball down the street at nearby Northeastern University. The Celtics retired his number (35) as a memorial to him.

These tragedies led to the Celtics compiling the worst record

The Celtics' fortunes worsened when Len Bias died two days after the 1986 NBA draft.

The drafting of Paul Pierce was another turning point in Celtics' history.

in seven years.

Pierce grew up in Inglewood, California, dreaming of playing for the Lakers. After an impressive career at the University of Kansas, though, he joined the Celtics. As soon as he arrived, Boston knew they had drafted the right guy. Pierce could score, rebound, defend, and come through in the clutch. One of the best ever to wear the green, Pierce is a 10-time All-Star. And he is one of only three Celtics, alongside Bird and Havlicek, who have scored over 20,000 points in their careers with the Celtics.

After Pierce torched the Lakers for 42 points one night, LA center

in the NBA (15-67) in 1996-97, their worst season in franchise history. But things began to turn around with the drafting of Pierce in 1998. More than anyone, Pierce was the reason for the Celtics returning to the playoffs in 2002, for the first time

Shaquille O'Neal pulled a Boston reporter aside. Shaq said, "Take this down. ...I knew he could play, but I didn't know he could play like this. Paul Pierce is 'The Truth.'"

But while "The Truth" was instrumental in returning the Celtics to the playoffs, he couldn't get them back to the Finals. Not by himself. That changed in the summer of 2007.

Lucky the Leprechaun had obviously returned from his vacation. Ainge, like Auerbach before him, made a series of moves. The most important: acquiring superstars Ray Allen from Seattle and Kevin Garnett from Minnesota. The Garnett deal, at seven

"The Truth"
Paul Pierce was the complete package: he could score, rebound, defend, and step up when it mattered most!

players for one, was the biggest trade in NBA history. And it immediately benefitted Boston.

Garnett and Allen were All-Stars in other cities, idling in Minnesota and Seattle, respectively. Their teams

The Celtics' GM Ainge chats with Coach Doc Rivers.

The "Boston Three Party"

Like the revolutionaries who threw tea into the Boston Harbor, Paul Pierce, Kevin Garnett, and Ray Allen caused all kinds of trouble for the rest of the league.

were going nowhere. With KG and Allen able to score, Pierce no longer had to carry the entire offense. He could focus on defense. As a result, the Celtics captured the NBA crown in their first year together. The three of them instantly bonded—and formed a trio for the ages.

But they didn't want to be called "The Big Three," the name given to Bird, McHale, and Parish two decades earlier. They liked the "Boston Three Party," created by ESPN.

Not long after the nickname was established, though, it became clear there was a fourth member of the party: All-Star point guard Rajon Rondo.

Rondo was raised by his mom in Louisville, Kentucky, who steered him away from football and toward basketball. She felt the sport would be less punishing on his skinny frame.

But she needn't have worried. Rondo is fearless. Just ask the Louisville fans he angered by signing to

Pierce, Garnett and Allen became known as the "Boston Three Party."

38

Rajon Rondo quickly established himself as the "Fourth Musketeer," proving that Boston had more than three superstars.

play at cross-state rival Kentucky. After two years with the Wildcats, he declared for the 2006 NBA Draft. Selected 21st overall by the Phoenix Suns, he was traded to the Celtics. He made his NBA debut as a rookie during the 2006–07 season.

Rondo played a supporting role before he established himself as the starting point guard for the Celtics during the 2007–08 championship season. His breakout performance came during the 2009 playoffs, where he helped the Celtics—without an injured Garnett—take the eventual Eastern-Conference champion Orlando Magic to seven games in the semifinals.

Since then, Rondo has taken his game to another level with his on-court leadership. Even the "Three Party" appeared to agree that they

Point Man

Rajon Rondo was so vital running the offense for Boston that he became the unofficial fourth member of the "Three Party." According to Coach Doc Rivers, he's the one dictating the success of today's Celtics.

As he matured on the court, Rondo proved that he was the key to the Celtics' success.

were just pieces in a puzzle—and that their point guard may just have become the biggest piece.

"Rajon's amazing, period," said Garnett. "We just have to make sure we follow his lead and follow his effort."

Rondo, although only 6'1", has a wingspan of 6'9" and hands that measure 9.5 inches long and 10 inches wide! These physical characteristics give him unique advantages on the court. Not only can Rondo catch a rebound one-handed and start the break in mid-air, but he is a defensive force. Rondo is equally adept at blocking shots on the perimeter as he is making steals.

Boston Coach Doc Rivers was a top-notch point guard himself for many years in the NBA. He gave

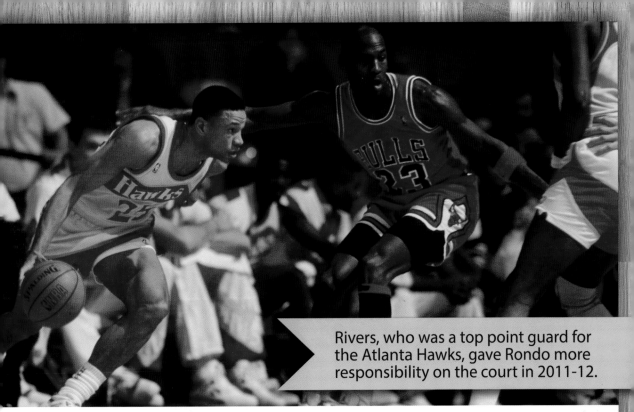

Rivers, who was a top point guard for the Atlanta Hawks, gave Rondo more responsibility on the court in 2011-12.

Rondo more responsibility with the ball on the floor during the 2011-12 season. Such a move ensured that Rondo would be the one dictating the success of a veteran Celtic team.

"They understand Rondo is the leader of the team. Everybody else plays with Rondo," said Rivers. "Kevin is still a great player. Paul is still our best scorer. They've kind of gotten out of each other's way with roles."

Unfortunately, Rondo suffered a torn ACL in a game against Atlanta in January 2013, ending his season -- and possibly Boston's as well.

"We still like our chances in the Eastern Conference," said Pierce.

"You can write the obituary," added Rivers. "But I'm not."

Chapter 5
More Banners...?

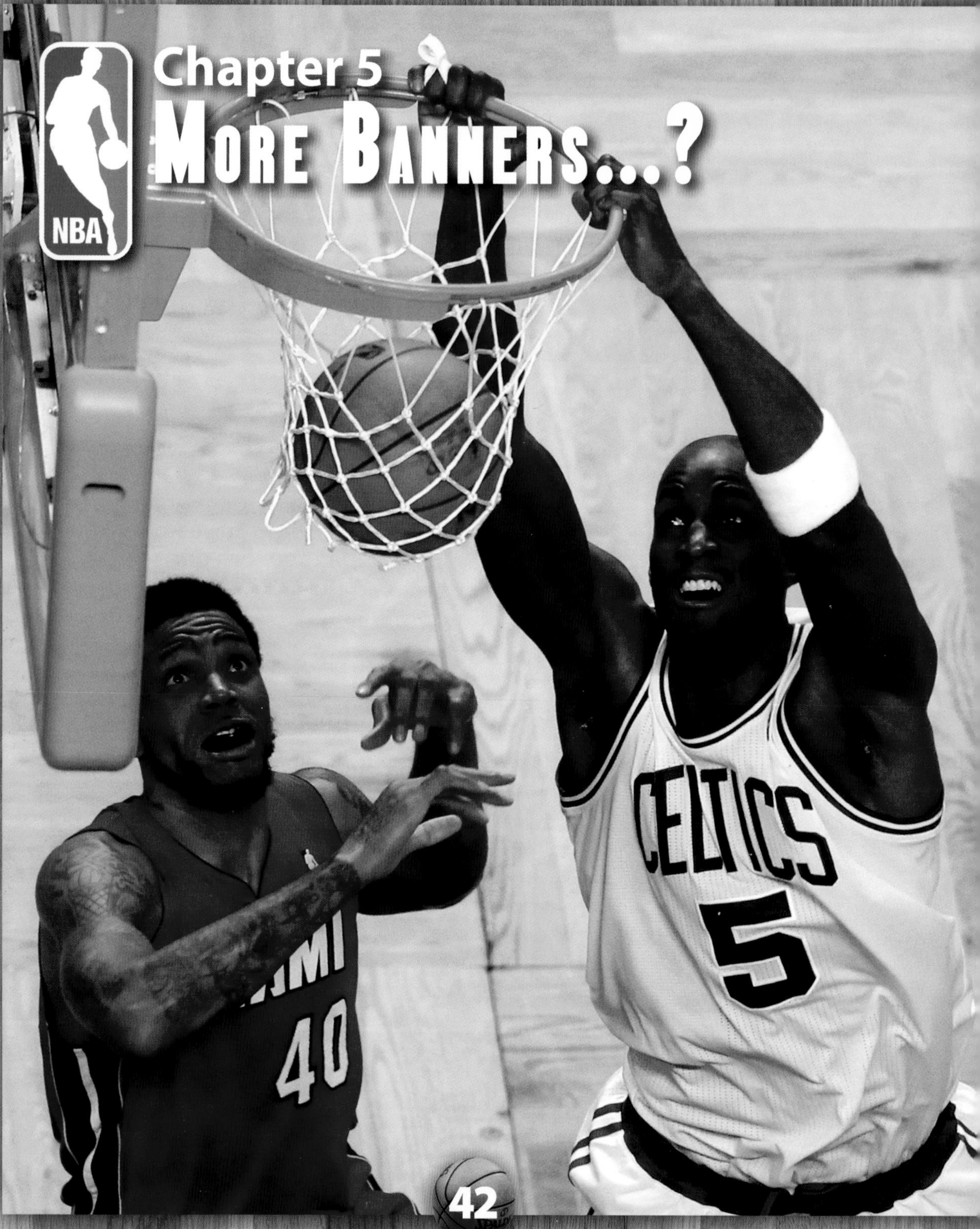

The Celtics—and their fans—were determined to repeat as world champions in 2009. Pierce missed only one game the entire year and led the team in scoring. But a knee injury to Garnett forced him to miss the final 25 games of the regular season and the entire playoffs. The Celtics ended up losing in the second round to Orlando.

They came back in 2010 set on returning to the NBA Finals. In Game 3 of the first round of the playoffs, Pierce hit a 21-foot jumper at the buzzer to beat Miami, 100–98, and give the Celtics a 3–0 series lead. The Celtics went on to win that series, and also defeated the heavily favored Cavaliers in the second round. They beat the Magic in six games in the Eastern Conference Finals to advance to their second Finals appearance in the "Three Party" era.

Just like a Hollywood script, they faced off against the Lakers in

Pierce nailed this 21-foot jumper at the buzzer to give the Celtics a 100-98 win over the Miami Heat.

When the Celtics squared off against the Lakers in the 2010 Finals, it was the continuation of the greatest rivalry in NBA history.

Second Thoughts

After the Lakers beat the Celtics in the 2010 NBA Finals, Rivers thought about retiring. But he returned to try to bring glory back to Boston.

a rematch of the 2008 Finals. It was the 12th time the two teams met for the championship. After taking a 3-2 lead, the Celtics headed back to Los Angeles, only to get blown out in Game 6.

It all came down to Game 7 in the Staples Center. It looked like Boston was going to deny LA their back-to-back title, but the Celtics blew a 13-point lead and lost, 83-79.

After the series, Rivers thought about leaving the bench to spend more time with his family. But he decided to honor the last year of his contract and return for the 2010-11 season. Then, after months of rumors that he would retire, the Celtics and Rivers agreed on a five-year contract extension.

In 2012, the Celtics came just one win away from making their third NBA Finals appearances since 2008. With the Eastern Conference Finals tied at two games apiece, Pierce drained a three-pointer with less than a minute to go to give the Celtics the win over Miami in Game 5. But the Heat, behind 45 points from LeBron James, ensured the series would go the distance. A 98–79 blowout win at Boston sent the series back to Miami for a seventh and deciding game.

In Game 7, the Celtics started strong and had a seven-point lead at halftime. But the Heat battled back

The Celtics gave the Heat all they could handle in the 2012 NBA playoffs but came up short.

to tie it up after three. The Celtics had a one-point lead with eight minutes left in the game when James threw down a monster jam. Moments later, a Chris Bosh three-pointer gave the Heat the lead for good. The Celtics couldn't recover and lost, 101–88.

Rivers wants his players to think about the Heat all the time, as Miami is the team to beat in the Eastern Conference.

acquired All-Stars Dwight Howard and Steve Nash. Sportswriters hoping to play up the LA-Boston rivalry even more smelled blood. They swamped Rivers with questions about what those acquisitions meant for the Celtics.

"Honestly, I don't care about the Lakers," Rivers said. "I have my eye squarely on Miami. I come up to my players during the year. I bring up Miami every single day to them. I want them to hate them. I want them to beat them. That's gotta be our focus."

It was such a combative series that Rondo and Garnett walked off the court without shaking any of the Heat's hands.

With the bitter taste of defeat still in their mouths, the Celtics then had to watch as the Lakers

Should the Lakers be their opponent in the Finals yet again, so be it. Boston first needs to get past Miami—with the Heat's own "Big Three" of James, Bosh, and Dwayne Wade. And there's more. Allen became a free agent and took less money than Boston offered to join them in Miami. The stage was set when Boston traveled to South Beach to open up the 2012-13 season—on the night the Heat got their championship rings.

All things considered, the Celtics really don't need any additional motivation from their coach. Besides, the most legendary franchise in the NBA has always risen to the occasion—even when their leprechaun leaves for vacation, as it appears he did once again on the night Rondo was injured.

So Rivers, Garnett, Pierce, and a core of young and talented guards (Jason Terry, Courtney Lee, and Avery Bradley) will need some more Celtic magic if they want to hang another banner in the Garden.

They'll be sure to find the room.

There's always room for another championship banner in the TD Garden.